I'm Still Making Money With Binary Options – And You Can Too!

José Manuel Moreira Batista

"I was looking for something that would really help me make money with binary options. This is a book that totally exceeded my expectations." – *Kina*

"Great reality check. The part about how not to be a fool and get screwed by your broker is alone worth the price of the book." – *Renko*

"Superb book. Honest information about this field. Great money management tips. Beginners can start trading immediately with the time-based strategies presented, they are very straightforward. The Advanced Strategies section is a different matter: you'll really have to put your mind to work to understand them." – *W. Chen*

"I'm amazed! This book actually discloses specific trading strategies that can be put to work immediately." – *Paul*

"This is the best information I ever came across. Five stars!" – *Harry C.*

INTRODUCTION

The objective of this book is to teach you a way of thinking about trading and more specifically a way of thinking about trading binary options. It will provide you with the mindset and a methodology that you can use by yourself to analyze opportunities in the binary options field. We will be covering strategies that are very well suited to trading binary options. But you will get out of this book more than just a set of specific strategies, you will learn the correct way to approach trading and what the pitfalls of trading binary options are.

This book does not assume any prior knowledge. If you know nothing about binary options then you can just start at the beginning and proceed. If you do know something or even a lot about trading or binary options it may well be that you are tempted to skip some sections but please don't. By doing so you might lose some perspective or some information that you are unaware of. Rest assured that there is no fluff in this book - you will not be wasting your time and by reading through at the very least you will be refreshing your knowledge. Another good reason to follow the book from beginning to end is that it will increase in difficulty gradually in a planned way. If you jump ahead and just go straight to the last sections, you are probably in for a needless shock. That will not happen if you just follow the path presented in the book. So, start at very beginning and gradually progress to the end. And when you get there remember to claim your reader bonus.

Trade with common sense, have fun and make profits!

José Manuel Moreira Batista

Table of Contents

Binary options 101s

In the United States of America when a course is called 101 it means it is a very basic course. These are important courses because they introduce the basic terminology and concepts that have to be understood and mastered before more complex issues may be pursued. This section of the book is thus called 101 because it aims to give you the language and essential body of knowledge about binary options. The S stands for secrets, because here we will cover things that are not usually taught in courses or books about binary options.

Definitions

What is a *binary option*? It is simply a way to speculate if the price of an asset is going to go up or down in the future during a certain time period. There are several binary option types but the core idea behind all of them is the same: choose an asset, pick a time horizon and guess what will happen to the price of that asset during that period. If your forecast is correct, you will earn a seemingly considerable return more often than north of 70%. If your prediction is wrong, you will lose the price you paid for the binary option contract that is you will in fact lose 100% of your stake.

Terminology

Stake refers to the amount of money you invest. Actually some people say they *invest* in binary options, other say that they *trade* binary options, and still others say that they *bet*, *wager* or *speculate* in binary options. For me, these are all the same, I make no distinction whatsoever as I'm not really into semantics.

Now, *asset* is a term I use to refer to anything that can be speculated on with binary options, such as the price of gold, the price of a share of a company, a currency pair or a stock market index.

Options are contracts

An *option* is a very old financial instrument and it can be used both for hedging and speculation purposes. It gives the *holder* of the option, the right but not the obligation to buy or sell an *underlying asset* at the specified price until a certain day called the *expiration date*. The value of an option depends on both the value of the underlying asset and the time remaining until the expiration date. Options are an essential component of the financial world: more than 20 billion dollars of options and futures contracts are traded every year.

Traditional users of options contracts are farmers. Wanting to protect the selling price of a crop that they will be able to sell only in four or five months' time they buy an option contract that guarantees them a minimum selling price. The owner of a factory that uses the farmers' crop as input in its production process has an opposite goal. The factory owner wants to put a ceiling on the maximum price of their input so he buys an option contract that guarantees him a maximum buying price. Although countless of buyers and sellers with a real need for options contracts do exist, most of the contracts are traded by speculators. They provide an essential function to the market by assuring its liquidity. Speculators don't want to protect the price of an input or output, they just want to make money. The fact is, without the speculators, buyers and sellers of options contract would have a very tough time finding one another. Speculators are critical, even essential for the financial world to function properly.

Binary options are but a very simplified version of the options contract that are traded in the stock and futures exchanges around the world. The word *binary* refers to the only two possible outcomes of buying this type of option: either you will lose all the money you have bet or you will keep it and earn a substantial return on top of it.

Exchange traded options

In order to fully understand the field of binary options, it is critical to make a distinction between exchange traded options and over the counter options. As the name implies, an exchange traded option is one that is traded on an exchange, meaning a marketplace which is public, has a supervisory board and is subject to rules and regulations. One of the world's largest exchanges is the Chicago Board of Options Exchange. It does offer binary options, one on the S&P 500 index and another one on the Volatility index. The end value of these contracts varies between 0 for an unsuccessful trade and 100 dollars for a successful one. If you want to buy one of these contracts you will have to find another trader that is willing to sell it to you; if you want to sell one then you will have to find a trader who wants to buy it. It works just as if you were trading Apple or BMW shares. Most of the binary options brokers <u>do not</u> work this way and do not offer these standardized options contracts that are traded on an exchange, which is public and is subject to known rules and regulations.

A brief review

Most binary options brokers work with OTC or over the counter options. What this means is that when you trade, it is your broker that is your trading counterpart. It might occur from time to time that when you open a position another trader opens the exact opposite trade, but this happens by chance and not by design. Contrast this situation with what happens in the stock market: if you give your broker an order to buy 100 shares of Amazon, that order is only executed if and when another trader wants to sell you those shares. Your stockbroker couldn't care less if the price of Amazon goes up or down, he will be happy to receive a matchmaking fee. In the OTC binary options arena, your broker will act as your counterpart and therefore he will be assuming a trade risk. Since his business is brokerage and not trading, he will try to get rid of that risk. He has two main ways of accomplishing that objective. One way is to balance his positions: he could try to be position neutral by having the same number of contracts on each side of the trade. That will be very, very, very hard to pull out but just for the sake of argument let's assume that he does achieve that goal. In that case, regardless of how the asset performs until the expiration date, he does not win or lose. That's good for him, isn't it? But wait a minute! Something seems to be missing... Since he does not charge a commission, how does he earn money with the trade? To answer that question, we are going to refresh our knowledge about the grandfather of modern betting: the coin tossing game.

Coin tossing and binary options

The coin tossing game, simple as it is, offers an invaluable insight to traders. Let's have a look. Suppose I offer you the chance of participating in a coin tossing game. You must bet 1 euro and you are free to choose the side of the coin that will give you a win. If you lose the bet you will lose your 1 euro. What is the minimum payout that would make you enter this game? Let's analyze this problem step by step. Asking for the minimum acceptable bet payout is really asking for the conditions that would make this a fair bet, isn't it? By definition a fair bet is one where you have equal chances of winning or losing the same amount. Let's assume that you pick heads. What is the probability of heads landing up? I guess you say it's 50% and that it is the same probability of tails coming up. You're right of course, but how do you know, how did you reach that conclusion? If you think about it you will realize that you are making a number of assumptions. You for instance assuming that the coin is a balanced coin, that is has not been doctored to land more often on one side than on the other. That seems to be a good assumption as I offered you the choice of picking the winning side, but then how do you know that a balanced coin has a 50% chance of landing on any one of its sides? Well, you know because the coin has only two sides, so it can only land heads or tails and everybody knows that this translates into a 50% chance. Come to think of it, a coin can conceivably land straight up, but the probability of that happening is so small that we can safely ignore it. Actually, that is a classic example of an event that may happen but has a zero probability of occurring. Back to heads and tails, how does everybody know that each side of a coin has a 50% chance of showing up? I guess that came about because a lot of people have been tossing coins for the past centuries and these people took notice of what happened. A few of them even took the trouble to register their coin tossing experiences very meticulously. That process generated lots of patterns, from which reliable statistics were calculated. It was all that data and all those calculations that lead us to the firm conclusion that a balanced coin when tossed will show heads up 50% of the time and of course it will also show tails up about 50% of the time.

Betting on a coin toss

Now that we have established that the fair coin tossing game has a 50% chance of winning, what is the minimum payout that you would accept to play the game if the stake is 1 euro? You have a 50% chance of losing your stake and you have a 50% chance of winning a payout which is the stake plus a return. Logically, you will only accept to play if your expected win at least equals your expected loss. When the expected win equals the expected loss everything depends purely on luck. To win you will have to be lucky but to lose you will have to be unlucky. If the expected win is less than the expected loss, you will lose money in the long run no matter how lucky you are. If the expected win exceeds the expected loss you will make money in the long run no matter how unlucky you are. So, what is the payout that makes the expected win to be equal to the expected loss? That's easy, we just have to write down what we just said as an equation. So 50% times 1 euro has to be equal to 50% times the return in case of win.

50% x 1 euro = 50% x return

Clearly this is to say that the return has to be equal to 1 euro. Voilà! To accept playing the coin tossing game you require a minimum return of 1 euro which is to say a payout of 2 euros. You stake 1 euro and if you lose your loss is 1 euro. If you win you get your original stake of 1 euro back plus a return of 1 euro which is the same as to say you will receive a payout of 2 euros.

How does a 90% return sounds to you now?

Okay my friend, here is what I proposed we do, we are going to play a coin tossing game with a coin of your own choosing. You are going to stake 1 euro or whatever the amount you fancy and if you win I'm going to pay you a 90% return. Great isn't it? What do you say? Shall we start? What's that? You're not interested? Not fair, says you? Well, let me ask you another question then. If you find that the 90% return is not good enough for you because the coin tossing game would not be fair, why would you enter a 60 second binary options contract that pays you a 70% return? Or for that matter why would you enter any binary options contract for any duration if it pays less than a 100% return? I submit there are only two reasons that could justify entering such a bet. First, you are in for the excitement and the entertainment just as if you were in a casino. Making money is not your main goal, having fun is and that is perfectly okay. I for sure am all in favor of people having fun and even to spend all their money in the process provided it is really their money. The second conceivable reason to accepting that bet is that you know more than the other fellow. In other words, you have a system and that system gives you an edge. Your chance of winning is not 50%, it is higher. The thing is, to develop such a system requires significant historical data to develop hypothesis and to test them. Do you have access to the required historical data for the asset you are planning to bet on? Does that data match the timeframe you intend to trade on? If you are like 99% of the people who are into binary options, you don't have the data let alone the tested system that produces the necessary above average results. If you are in for the fun by all means go for it. But if your goal is to make money, that's not the way to approach it.

Tom won 5000 euros with a 60-second bet!

Anecdotal evidence has a way to insinuate itself in the conversation at this juncture. Chances are you have a friend or acquaintance who knows about a guy, let's called him Tom, who just won 5000 euros on a 60-second bet. Lucky Tom acted on a tip he received from his nice account manager at FabulousBinaryOptionsBroker.com or from a talking head he watched on CNBC. He struck gold and he is hooked and he tells everybody and his cousin that binary options is the way to go. The reality is, he really had the same 50% chance of winning those 5000 euros as he did of losing the 7000 euros he invested in the contract. Tom is guaranteed to lose money if he keeps on betting just as he would if he were in a casino. If Tom takes his win and run, that's another matter, then he really would have made good money. Unfortunately a vicious virus called greed has by this time probably infected Tom and it is much more likely that he goes on betting and ends up losing more than the 5000 euros he won. The vast majority of people who win by sheer luck continue to bet until they have lost all their gains and then some. Behavioral economist have studied this phenomena extensively. It seems that we are very, very good at taking the credit for our random wins and blaming bad luck and other external factors for our losses. Plus, you can be sure that after each one of Tom's wins, his friendly account manager will give him a call to congratulate him for his shrewdness and uncanny trading ability. And did he know about this upcoming big event next week? Yep, Tom is bound to make a bundle on that one and his account manager will make sure he gets serious this time and really bets big. No more measly 5000 euros bets. By the way, did Tom tell you about the extraordinary bonus he was able to get because he funded his account with just 10000 euros? That's right, he funded his account with the paltry sum of 10000 euros and his friendly account manager pestered her boss until he bent over and credited Tom's account with a matching amount. Tom now has 20000 euros to invest, isn't that something? With all his new found skill and trading competence he will soon grow that to 1 million euros. He will then retire to Paradise Island where he plans to continue to bet on binary options on a part-time basis to grow his vast fortune. What's that you're asking? No, there were no strings attached to the funding bonus... Well, there is a minimum number of trades that have to be completed before any money can be withdrawn from the broker but as Tom plans to continue investing anyway to compound his wins that does not count. Does it? Time for a reality check: with most binary brokers it is much easier to put money in than it is to take money out. If you think that you can withdraw money from your broker with a simple keyboard click then you may be in for a rough surprise. As soon as you put in your online withdrawal request, chances are you will be getting a call from your account manager and guess what? He has a super tip for you, maybe even coupled with a fantastic new bonus. You have been making money haven't you, why would you even consider doing such a stupid thing as forfeiting your opportunity to make even more money? Remember the Roach Motel? Yeah, it's easy to check in but you can never check out.

Artificial Intelligence to the rescue!

Chances are someone reading this book is now thinking along these lines:

"You know what Jose, I don't really care about anything you just said about historical data and testing and probabilities of winning and losing and all that mind-numbing stuff. I just bought myself the most powerful trading robot ever devised, it runs on Artificial Intelligence 3.0, it flashes buy and sell signals and its performance is awesome. I've seen the account statements; this baby generates profits faster than you can say "crossing moving averages"! It works 24 hours per day, it trades all forex pairs on all time frames and I got it for a very special launching price of only 199 dollars."

Right. Hum... let's see, how shall I break it to you without yelling "You are a hopeless moron!"? These robots are made and sold by the affiliates of the brokers if not by the brokers themselves. The affiliates get commissions on the funding amounts and on the trading spreads. Those robots are conceived with just one big objective in mind: to make you trade a lot. The account statements when not totally made up simply show the carefully selected periods when by pure chance the robots scored more wins that losses. Don't believe me? Just read their disclaimer. You can't miss it: it's a compact, very small light gray text shown over white background that will make you think that your doctor prescribed you the wrong eyeglasses.

Sine qua non

Sine qua non is Latin for stuff you really need to have and this is what this section is about: the three pillars of effective trading. The first pillar is historical data: you absolutely need historical data to look for patterns, to come up with ideas for trading systems and to test them. The second pillar is trading systems. You will need at least one trading system, preferably more. And you need that these systems have a positive expectancy. Last but not the least you need an effective money management system. Lots of trading systems break down because they are not coupled with an adequate money management. A poor trading system will always be a poor trading system but it can turn into a nightmarish money sinking monster if you have not an effective money management system. On the other hand a good trading system might produce dismal or even negative results if it lacks the support of sound money management.

Historical data

If you really want to start trading seriously, to approach it in a professional way and not merely to have fun, the first thing that you need is historical data. Why? Because in the financial world, extrapolating form the past is the only known way to make systematic predictions. You therefore need to have the data corresponding yo the assets you are going to trade and you need that data for the time frame that you are intending to trade. Suppose that you are intending to trade hourly. A set of weekly or daily data won't do you any good because hourly is a shorter time frame and you will have no relevant information. Now if you have daily data you can build weekly, monthly, quarterly or yearly data. You can work with data that refers to a shorter time frame and compress it to longer time frames but the opposite is not true. You cannot from daily data extrapolate hourly data, nor can you from hourly data extrapolate minute data so you need at least to have the data corresponding to the time frame you want to trade in. However this data collecting business is much more complex and generates much more errors than you might think, so quality data does not come about easily nor is it cheap.

Moreover, the shorter the time frame the more *noise* your data will have. Noise refers to variations that are actually random and this noise has only one function: it is put there by Mister Market to screw up your analysis. If you want a good piece of advice this is it: stick to longer time frames, not only will the data be more meaningful but you might actually get it for free. What do I mean by higher time frame? I mean daily. If you stick to the daily time frame you will be able to download a lot of data which albeit not excellent will do and has the added advantage of being free. Yahoo and Dukascopy are two known sites that provide free daily data.

A trading system

Let's talk about trading systems. What is a trading system? At its most basic, a trading system is but a set of rules: rules to enter a position and rules to exit that position. That is all that is needed to build a trading system. Sure, there are very sophisticated and complex trading systems but even those have a set of rules to enter a position and a set of rules to exit that position. Of particular interest for binary options traders are time-based strategies. These are strategies that require you to open a trade at a certain date and to close it also at a certain date. Both dates are known before entering the trade.

Positive expectancy

Once you have data and a trading strategy, you want to make sure that your trading strategy has a positive *expectancy*. What is expectancy? Expectancy is a number, a very important number to any trader. If a strategy's expectancy is a negative, you shouldn't trade that strategy. If a strategy's expectancy is positive then it's okay to trade that strategy. A strategy with a positive expectancy will make money in the long run and a strategy with a negative expectancy will lose money in the long run. It couldn't be any easier than this. You can use expectancy to assess the worthiness of a trading strategy and you can use it to rank strategies. For example if both strategy A and strategy B have a positive expectancy, which one should you trade? Answer: the one with a higher expectancy. Simple, isn't it?

How to calculate a strategy's Expectancy

How do we calculate a strategy's expectancy? Let's go over it step by step. The first step is to calculate strategy's *win ratio*. What is the win ratio? It's nothing but its historical success rate. To put it in other words, it is the percentage of times that a strategy wins:

Win ratio = Number of wins / number of trades

This will result in a decimal number such as 0,60 or 0,653. To express the result as a percentage you just multiply it by 100. In that way 0,60 is shown as 60% and 0,653 as 65,3%. Having calculated the win ratio, we can now easily calculate the *loss ratio*. To do that we just subtract the win ratio from 1.

Loss ratio = 1 – win ratio

For example, for a win ratio of 60% we get a win ratio of 0,40 or 40%. Notice the unbeatable logic: as there are only those two possible outcomes, if a trading strategy wins 60% of the time, it will lose 40% of the time. If it wins 70% of the time then it will lose 30% of the time. Next we need to calculate the *reward to risk ratio*. Fancy name, don't you agree? The reward to risk ratio is exactly what the name implies, it shows how much you expect to win per unit of money that you are risk losing. In other words, you first find out how much on average do you win when the strategy wins; and then you find out how much on average do you lose when the strategy loses. You then compare these two amounts. To calculate this ratio you divide the average win amount of your strategy by its average loss amount.

Reward to risk = average win ÷ average loss

Finally, to get the strategy's expectancy you just multiply the reward to risk ratio by the win ratio and then subtract the loss ratio:

Expectancy = reward to risk X win ratio – loss ratio

Expectancy calculation example

Let's use an example to go over the calculations. Suppose you have a strategy that wins 65% of the trades. A win yields a profit of 72 euros and a loss sets you back by 100 euros. The loss ratio is obviously 35% or 100% minus 65%. The reward to risk ratio is obtained dividing the average win amount of 72 euros by the average loss of 100 euros. That turns out to be 0,72. The expectancy of this strategy is given by:

Expectancy = 0,72 X 0,65 – 0,35

That turns out to be 0,118. It is a positive number signaling a strategy worth using. Notice that a reward to risk ratio of 0,72 is common when trading binary options: you get a 72% return if your trade is successful and you lose 100% of your bet if it fails.

A money management system

The last one of our three sine qua non components of sound trading is a money management system. The main objective of such a system is to make sure that we don't blow up all our money in a few trades. However, a good management system can actually improve our trading performance by a lot. So we look for a money management system both to protect our downside and to boost our trading performance.

The Kelly criterion

John Larry Kelly was a scientist, a physician that worked at Bell Labs in the fifties when it was a cutting edge research outfit. Kelly was not only very, very smart, he doubled up as a recreational gun-slinger and dare-devil pilot. On his free time he developed what became known as the Kelly Criterion or Kelly Formula or simply the Kelly Percentage. The formula tells you what exactly is the percentage of your trading capital that you should stake on each trade in order to maximize the rate of growth of your money.

$$\text{Kelly \%} = [\text{win ratio} \times (\text{average win return} + 1) - 1] / \text{average win return}$$

With the same data we used before to exemplify the calculation of expectancy,

$$\text{Kelly \%} = (0,65 \times (0,72 + 1) - 1) / 0,72$$

That turns out to be 0,1639 which is to say 16,39% or roughly 16%. This means that if your trading capital is 1000 euros, on that trade you should bet 16% or 160 euros. If your trading capital is 500 euros, you should wager 16% of 500 euros or 80 euros. Note that even if you trade always the same strategy you must recalculate the amount to bet after each trade because your capital changes. Of course if you change strategy or if the win ratio or the average return of the strategy changes, you will also have to recalculate since the Kelly % itself will be different.

How is your blood pressure?

At this point a warning is in order: the Kelly Criterion is not for the faint hearted. You will experience significant drawdowns in your bankroll if you use it. The fact that it is the proven best system to grow your capital does not mean that you will have a smooth ride. Quite the opposite, it will be a tough voyage so if you are unsure about your ability to cope, use a half-Kelly or even a quarter-Kelly. This means using only half the percentage or a quarter of the percentage that you calculate with the Kelly Formula. For example if the Kelly % is 16% using a half-Kelly you would only stake 8% of your capital; using a quarter-Kelly which is what I recommend you do, you would bet 4% of your capital. This reduced bet amounts will slow the rate of growth of your capital but at the same time they will substantially decrease the chances of you having to pay an unwanted visit to the emergency room with an anxiety attack or worse. An additional and very important point: regardless of how tough you are or how high your risk tolerance is, do not ever bet a percentage of your capital higher than the Kelly Percentage. That is mathematically proven to be the fastest way there is to lose all your money.

The second best money management system is arguably the Percentage of Bankroll. With it you simply bet a fixed percentage of your trading capital, or bankroll, on each trade. That percentage varies between 2% to 5%, with 2% being the most frequently recommended value. If you have 1000 euros, you bet 20 euros. If you have but 500 euros, you wager 10 euros.

Time-based strategies

In this section we will go over 6 time-based strategies. Time-based strategies are particularly suitable to trading binary options since they open and close a position at specific and known beforehand times. In other words for time-based strategies we do not need to watch out for technical formations, we don't even need to be looking at charts, we ignore indicators and we couldn't care less about the news. The only tool we need is a calendar. With any one of these strategies, we have but two simple instructions to follow: "open on day X", "close on day Y". This is about as simple as it gets.

The Calends

This strategy derives its name from the ancient Romans. They called the first day of each month of their calendar the Calends. Based on the idea that each calendar month has its own trading seasonality, the Calends strategy tries to profit by identifying recurring monthly upwards or downwards pricing patterns. It goes about it by comparing, for each calendar month, the opening price of the first trading day with the closing price of the last trading day. This is repeated for all the years for which there is data. Finally, for each calendar month, one looks at the tally. If it shows that the closing price is more often above than below the opening price, that month's trade will be to buy a *bullish* binary options contract. A bullish trade is one that wins if the asset price rises for the time period. On the other hand, if the tally shows that the closing price is more often below than above the opening price, that month's trade will be to buy a *bearish* binary options contract. A bearish trade is one that wins if the asset price falls.

Let's review this process again, because its rationale will be applied not only for this strategy but for all the other strategies. We begin by looking at what happened in the past for the asset and for the time-frame which interest us. What has happened more often? Did the price rise more often than it fell? Or did it fall more often than it rose? The answer to this question will give us the direction of the trade. After that we have to calculate the trade's expectancy. We only trade if the trade's expectancy is positive. That's our iron clad criterion. We will go through examples later on but for now let's have a look at the next strategy in our arsenal.

The Four Seasons

The four seasons of the year, winter, spring, summer and fall result from the revolution of the earth around the sun. Each one of these seasons has its own weather patterns and daylight hours. They are often associated with mood changes that a lot of people believe have a significant impact on the economy, on commerce and on trading. Corporations report earnings and business outlooks on a quarterly basis, and this often coincides with the shifting of large amounts of money around the world. All this has surely an impact on stock prices, on index prices and on exchange rates. The Four Seasons strategy builds on these patterns. Operationally it considers the year to be divided into four 3-months periods: winter goes from January to March; spring from April to June; summer from July to September; and fall from October to December. We look at what happened more often in the past to determine if we are going to put on bullish or bearish trades. These trades are to be opened on the first trading day of the season and they are to be closed at the last trading day of the season. Again, we only actually put on trades if their expectancy is positive.

Triple Witching Weeks

Traditional stock options expire on the third Friday of each month but four times a year in March, June, September and December the third Friday is also the expiration date of index options and futures. Traders refer to those as Triple Witching Weeks. They are often characterized by heightened volatility as traders close, roll over and open a substantial number of positions. This strategy aims to profit from the volatility that occurs during those Triple Witching weeks by opening a position on Monday and closing it on Friday. As before we start by checking what happened in the past. If from Monday to Friday the asset that we chose has risen more often than it has fallen, we have a potential bullish binary options trade. If the reverse has happened, we consider a bearish binary options trade. We have green light to trade when expectancy is positive.

Thanksgiving

Thanksgiving is that turkey eating season when Americans crisscross their country to stay with those relatives they can only endure for short periods of time. Relying on the bullish holiday spirits, the Thanksgiving strategy calls for buying at the open on the Monday before Thanksgiving day and exiting the trade at the close on the following Friday. People say Thanksgiving originates bullish trades but we don't go by what people say, we look at the facts. If in the past for the asset price has risen more often that it has fallen, we have a potential bullish trade. On the contrary if it has fallen more often that it has risen then we have a potential bearish trade.

Sell in May and Go Away

Sell in May and Go Away is perhaps Wall Street's most famous mantra. Historically, stocks have underperformed during the six-month period that goes from May to October. This strategy calls for opening a position at the beginning of November and closing it at the end of April. Although the trade is expected to be bullish, we again let what actually happened in the past to be our guide. This trade has a very long time-frame so it requires a lot of patience, a quality traders rarely have. Most brokers won't offer you the chance to play such a long time-frame strategy. Remember, the shorter the time-frame the more difficult it is for you to pick up meaningful recurring patterns. That's why the brokers like the short time-frames, and the shorter the better: they increase their edge over you.

January barometer

The January barometer is another long time-frame strategy. It was originally conceived by Yale Hirsch of Stock Trader's Almanac fame and it was intended to be used with the S&P 500 index. The strategy postulates the following: if the price of the asset rises in January, it will rise from February to December; if the price falls in January, it will fall from February to December. Again, we don't rely on postulates or sayings, we check to see what really happened in the past, we apply the expectancy filter and we act accordingly. A final remark: notice how a strategy that was initially built with one particular asset in mind can be tested and eventually used with a different asset. The key idea here is *test*. Always test. It is perfectly fine to pick an idea in one particular area and transpose it to another area, just don't do it blindly. Test and filter with expectancy. You might find out or already know about some other strategy devised for a particular asset or time-frame. If you want to apply it to trading binary options, all you have to do is to follow the methodology that we have been describing here. If the trade's expectancy is positive then go for it.

The setup

Relax, this is about gearing you up...In this section we will talk about finding the data you need for developing and testing your trading ideas, and were to get it for free. Next we will talk about contracts: what are the contracts available for you to trade, and which are the contracts best suited to apply the time-based trading strategies we discussed. Finally we will talk about the very important topic of broker selection. We will review the criteria, the questions you might want to consider and have answered before you trust your money to a broker. So this will be all about your setup, the things that you need to have in place before you actually start trading to make money: data, contracts and broker.

The data

You can easily find any kind of data on the internet if money is not an issue for you. Free data is another matter. If you are focusing mainly on stocks and stocks indices then Yahoo! Finance is probably your best choice. It offers free end of the day data, meaning the open, high, low and close price for each day. Downloading a single asset price history from Yahoo! Finance is a piece of cake but if you are going to download a lot of data you will need another approach. I use and recommend an inexpensive piece of software called MLDownloader. If you are a Mac user consider StockXloader. Historical data for forex and commodities are not available from Yahoo! Finance. If that is your focus have a look at Tick Data Downloader. This is a free piece of software that downloads the data directly from a broker called Dukascopy (no account needed). Downloading data for multiply currency pairs is a time consuming process that you might want to let your computer do while you're sleeping.

The contracts

Regarding the contracts to use, there are five which are very well suited to use with our time-based strategies. These are: Higher/Lower, Rise/Fall, Touch/No-Touch, Ends Between and Ends Outside and Stays Between and Goes Outside. The exact names of these contracts may differ from broker to broker but it is very easy to identify them. The names I'm using are from a broker called Binary.com. We will go over each contract in detail later on. My recommendation is that you master more than one contract and also that you be willing and prepared to trade more than one asset. This is because depending on the volatility in the market, brokers may temporarily make certain contracts or assets unavailable for trading. If you trade only one asset or one type of contract you might find yourself wanting to trade but being unable to do it because your broker simply doesn't allow you to make that specific trade at that time. You are thus better off if you have an understanding of several types of contracts and are prepared to trade in different types of assets.

The brokers

In this section I want to give you some pointers to help you decide with which broker or brokers you want to open an account. One of the very first things you might want to check is which assets are available to trade. Not all brokers make available the same assets to trade. Before you sign up with a broker check what his offering is, what assets and on what time-frames will you be able to trade. Contrary to what you might think, this is not always a straightforward task. A good dose of patience and persistence may be required. This is because broker platforms are really designed to make you sign-up with them, not to give you information. Be advised that signing-up for a demo account that requires disclosing your phone number just to get that basic information might not be a good idea. Doing so will put you at a serious risk of being pestered by a so-called account manager whose only job is to convince you to open a real account with real money.

Another thing that you want to know is how long the broker has been in operation. Brokers come and go a lot! True, the fact that a broker has been in operation for 5 years is no guarantee that he will be here next year. But the fact is that new brokers have to spend a lot of money in promotion. They have a lot of upfront expenses and they are focusing on attracting new customers and that's the most expensive type of marketing there is. Plus, while they are focusing on attracting new customers, there are not really tightening up their operations. They are more vulnerable to one-time events like the Swiss Franc appreciating 30% overnight and they might blow up much more easily than the older and savvier guys. They also tend to be underfunded. It is very easy miscalculate how much these things really cost in the beginning. So as a general remark, you might want to avoid brand new brokers and if it's really something that you want to get in, then get in with a very small amount of money.

Next, check available funding and withdrawal methods. For example, if you have an account with Skrill as I do, you want them to offer funding and withdrawal with Skrill as it adds an extra layer of security and convenience.

An important issue is the ease of withdrawal. Most of the brokers make it very easy for you to put money in but they can be a real pain in the neck when you want to take money out. The most reliable way to check this is to actually know someone who uses that broker and ask him what their experience was. Did you take money out? How much if you don't mind my asking? How long did it take? Did you have to call someone? Did you have to wait for someone to call you? Spend a little time satisfying yourself that the process is really seamless.

You also might want to consider if they'll give you a funding bonus. I personally am not a big fan of bonus because they tend to come with strings attached. However, if you are putting in only a small amount of money and if it is money that either you make it or you break it, money that you really don't mind losing, then it might make sense to accept a bonus that may substantially increase your trading capital.

Another consideration might be the existence of an affiliate program. Do they have an affiliate program? Chances are they do. So if you end up using that broker, if you really use and like that broker, making a little extra money by recommending the broker to other people makes sense.

Finally we come to what I call the pestering quotient of the broker. With some brokers as soon as you log in their platform, someone will call you. She will tell you she wants to help you make better trades. If you would just deposit a little more money in your account, she could put you in their VIP clients list. These VIP clients receive insider trading tips and advice and are guaranteed to make a bundle. Well, at least in my book this type of talk is a big no-no and reason enough not to open an account or close it immediately.

The playbook

In this section we will go over specific examples of the application of the time-based strategies we discussed to binary options trading. In these examples the S&P 500 index is the traded asset, but the methodology is what counts and it would work similarly with any other index, stock, forex pair or commodity.

The S&P 500 Index

Some brokers refer to the S&P 500 as the American index. It is a broad index of the most important publicly traded corporations in the United States. Its sticker on Yahoo! Finance is ^GSPC. That's where the data that I used to build the tables that you'll find in the examples came from.

Barrier contracts

Barrier contracts are perhaps the most commonly used binary options contracts. Let's see how they work. Again, I'm using the terminology of the broker Binary.com. Your broker may use a different name for these contracts but you won't have any difficulty in identifying them.

Higher / Lower

With the Higher/Lower barrier contract you pick either a duration or an end date or for the trade. For instance if it is the first day of March and you want to put on a trade that goes on until the end of the month you would choose either 31 days as the duration or March 31st as the end date. You also have to pick a barrier which is the reference price for the asset that you are trading. You are going to guess if the price of the asset at the close of the end date you have chosen is higher or lower than that barrier. Finally you have to choose how much you want as a payout or how much you want to stake in this trade. The stake is how much you pay to buy the contract, it is the amount of money that you put at risk. The payout is the stake plus the return, the amount of money that you will get if the trade is successful. With our system it is much easier to select how much to stake so that is what we are going to do.

Rise / Fall

The Rise/Fall contract is very similar to the Higher/Lower contract. In fact the only difference is that the barrier is the price of the asset at the time of trading, the *spot* price. You use the same data and statistics for the Rise/Fall contract that you use for the Higher/Lower contract.

Suppose for instance that the S&P500 opens at 2500 on March 1st and that your research shows that it should close higher on March 31st. If you are placing the Higher/Lower contract you set 2500 as your barrier. But suppose you want to buy a Rise/Fall contract and that by the time you log in to make your trade the S&P500 has fallen back to 2480. Is it okay to go ahead and place the Rise/Fall bet? Yes, because your original trade would be to bet that the S&P 500 would be higher than 2500 at the end of March. By placing the Rise/Fall bet with the spot price at 2480 you in fact have a cushion of 20 points. However, if the S&P500 spot price is at 2505 you should not trade. Why? Because your research indicates that the S&P500 should be higher than 2500, but it says nothing about it being higher than 2505. Think how you would feel if you went ahead and did the trade and the S&P500 closed on March 31st at 2502. Pretty bad, no? We never trade if we don't know and if we haven't tested it we do not know so we don't trade, period.

Trading the calends with a barrier contract

Before presenting specific examples you have to know that for my research I always assume that the return of a binary options contract is 70%. I found this to be a good cut-off level. If the actual return offered is above 70%, which happens more often than not, then I'm naturally okay with it since the trade's expectancy is really higher than what I'm assuming. If the return offered is below 70% I don't trade. I never, ever make an exception.

All the examples in this book use information from research available at the time of publication and are intended only for the purpose of explaining the application of the strategies. You should naturally make sure that you use updated research before engaging in trading. The section S&P500 research contains the data used in the examples.

The past performance of the S&P500 for the month of January summarizes as follows:

- The direction of the trade is *higher* because that's what happened 62,9% of the times in the past;
- The *expectancy* of the trade is 0,07 so it is okay to trade;
- The *Kelly %* is 10%;

Accordingly and supposing you have a bankroll of 1000 euros, you would buy a *higher* contract for the end of January setting as barrier the opening price of the S&P500 on the first trading day of January. You would stake 100 euros in this bet. That's the result of multiplying your bankroll of 1000 euros by the Kelly % of 10%. However, I strongly recommend that you do not use the full Kelly. Use only a half or a quarter-Kelly instead. I personally always try to place two completely different trades using a quarter-Kelly for each. For this trade I would therefore bet 25 euros and not 100 euros.

The four seasons

The past performance of the S&P500 for the quarter of January to March summarizes as follows:

- The direction of the trade is *higher* because that's what happened 60% of the times in the past;
- The *expectancy* of the trade is 0,02 so it is okay to trade;
- The *Kelly %* is 3%;

With a bankroll of 1000 euros we would stake 30 euros on this bet if using the full Kelly or 7,50 euros if going with the quarter/Kelly as I recommend.

June triple witching week

The past performance of the S&P500 for the June Triple Witching Week summarizes as follows:

- The direction of the trade is *higher* because that's what happened 53,7% of the times in the past;
- The *expectancy* of the trade is -0,09 so you should not trade;
- The *Kelly %* is 0%;

No bet is to be made under these circumstances. You might ask, what if they offered me not 70% but a 120% return? In that case you could recalculate the trade's expectancy and see if it turns out to be positive. As I want to keep things as automatic as possible, I always use the 70% return and if expectancy comes out negative I don't bet.

Thanksgiving

The past performance of the S&P500 for the Thanksgiving week summarizes as follows:

- The direction of the trade is *higher* because that's what happened 67,4% of the times in the past;
- The *expectancy* of the trade is 0,15 so it is okay to trade;
- The *Kelly %* is 21%;

With a bankroll of 1000 euros we would stake 210 euros on this bet if using the full Kelly or 52,50 euros if going with the quarter/Kelly as I recommend.

Sell in May and go away

The past performance of the S&P500 for the November to April period summarizes as follows:

- The direction of the trade is *higher* because that's what happened 74,4% of the times in the past;
- The *expectancy* of the trade is 0,27 so it is okay to trade;
- The *Kelly %* is 38%;

With a bankroll of 1000 euros we would stake 380 euros on this bet if using the full Kelly or 95 euros if going with the quarter/Kelly as I recommend.

Notice that the Kelly Formula is advising you to bet 38% of our capital. You can now better appreciate how using the full Kelly can result in an immediate big drawdown of your account.

January barometer

For the January Barometer we have to split our analysis in two. One for the higher direction and another one for the lower direction. You might remember that the January Barometer tells you that if the asset goes higher in January then it will also go higher for the remaining of the year. But if it goes lower in January it will also go lower for the remaining of the year.

Research confirms that when the index ends higher in January then from February to December it also ends higher 78.1% of the times. The trade's expectancy is a positive 0,33 and Kelly advises us to stake 47% of our capital. With a bankroll of 1000 euros, that would mean risking 470 euros in this single trade. Using the quarter-Kelly that amount would be 117,50 euros.

For the years when the index ended lower in January research shows it ended lower from February to December only 33.3% of the times. Expectancy turns out to be a negative -0,43 so no trade should be made.

Beyond the mechanics

This section is about some aspects that go beyond the mechanics of trading. These are issues that have to do with the psychology of trading and your attitude towards it. These are very important points because if you don't get these right everything else will fall apart and your long term prospects as a trader will suffer tremendously.

Bet stacking

Bet stacking refers to opening more than one bet at the same time and this can be done for good or bad reasons. If you open more than one bet because you lost one, two, three or four bets in a row, you are doing it for the wrong reasons and more likely than not will come to regret it. If you open more than one bet because you are searching for diversification you might be doing it for a very good reason. Let me give you some pointers if the latter is your case. First, as you already know, you should bet the amount that your money management system tells you to. That means that if you follow the percentage of bankroll system and you stake 2% on each bet, if you make four bets then you only allocate 0,5% to each bet. If you use the half-Kelly and the Kelly % is 5% if you make one bet you stake 2,5%. However, if you want to make not one but two bets you should stake only 1,25% on this specific bet. The general rule is that you calculate how much you would stake if you made only one bet and then divide that by the total number of bets you plan to do. Play defense with the money you allocate to each bet, always play defense. This brings us to another important theme, and that is watch out for correlation. What is correlation? It's the tendency of two assets to go together, to have the same price movement. Correlation is outside the scope of this book but as a general recommendation, try to make bets on different assets classes. For instance, place one bet in indexes, and place another one on the forex. If you are just betting on indexes, which is something I definitely advise you not to do, don't bet on the three North American indexes. Pick one from North America, one from Asia, and maybe one from Europe or from South America. If you concentrate your trades on the forex, avoid repeating currencies. Next, understand your bankroll. What I mean by this is that in your broker's account, you will one of two things or maybe both: cash and open positions. What is the value of your bankroll for the purpose of calculating the amount that you are going to stake on your next bet? Well, the cash component is easy because cash is worth its nominal value. If you have 750 euros in cash, count that as 750 euros. With regards to your open positions, your broker will most likely display a mysterious estimated value that you can safely ignore. Let me tell you the exact value you should consider for your open positions: zero, zilch, nada, niente. Or to phrase it differently, your bankroll value is equal to the amount of cash you have.

Losses are inevitable

Your attitude towards losses will greatly influence your performance as a trader. Understand that losses are inevitable. If you have a system that gives you a 70% win probability, and that is a very good system indeed, you in fact have a 30% loss probability. That means that the probability of losing your next bet is 30%. That is a high probability, you wouldn't go happily to surgery if you knew you had a 30% chance of dying. Notice further that with a 30% loss ratio the probability of losing twice in a row is 9% which is still high; the probability of losing three times in a row is 3% and the probability of losing 4 times in a row is 1%. Albeit small, these probabilities clearly show that losses will happen. You will suffer losses and you will more likely than not suffer rows of consecutive losses. Your money management system is there to help you especially when you find yourself facing consecutive losses. That is exactly the time when you should most trust your money management system. Don't ever abandon it. Don't double the stakes. Don't run after the money. Be patient and trust your money management system both when you are winning and especially when you suffer losses.

Long-term view

Your philosophy of trading should be based on a long term perspective. The short term view, you leave that to the people who go to the casino. The people who want to win the next second, they are there for the thrill, for the fun, for the enthusiasm, for the booze. They are the casino's owner dream clients. They have a great philosophy for entertainment but a lousy attitude for making money. Adopt the long term view, the Warren Buffet way, the one that is lousy for entertainment but that is very good for making money. Accept losses, stick to the system and know that tomorrow you will have the opportunity to place another trade. Don't be in a hurry to make trades. Only place trades that have a positive expectancy. Stick to your management system. Trust the long term view in order to make money consistently now and in the future.

Advanced strategies

In this section we are going to discuss two other types of contracts: *Touch* contracts and what I call *Lane* contracts. These contracts require more specialized knowledge. For starters we will have to cover the essentials of the normal distribution. Nothing too profound or complex, we just want to gain an operational understanding of a tool that will allow us to quantify and to test our strategies. That's the reason for the slightly menacing title of this section: Advanced Strategies. It is true that we will be required to think a little bit more deeply but it's really nothing too complicated. So without further ado, let's plunge into a brief overview of the normal distribution.

Normal distribution

The normal distribution is characterized by its bell shaped format and it reflects the most recurrent way that quantifiable data shows up in the world. For example, suppose that we are looking at the population of a village and that we want to study its weight pattern. The first thing we do is to take everyone's weight. We then sum all the weights and divide that sum by the total number of people. That of course gives us the mean or average weight of the people in that village. Suppose that mean is 80 kilos. That's a nice piece of concise information but in order to have a broader, more meaningful understanding of the data, we now measure how close or far away each individual is from that 80 kilos value. There is a tool for that called the *standard deviation*. It is usually represented by the Greek letter sigma (σ). Suppose that the standard deviation turns out to be 5 kilos. As we can safely assume that the weight of the individuals in the village is distributed according to the normal distribution we now have all the information we need to draw some pretty interesting conclusions.

Normal distribution

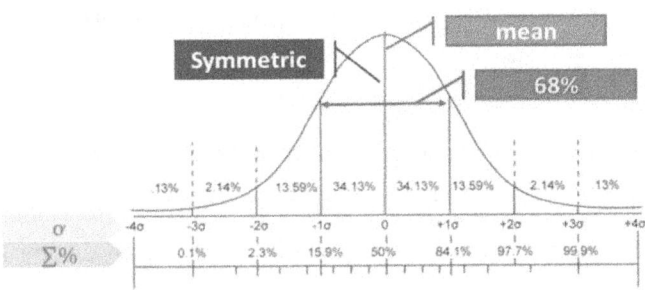

Look at the generic normal distribution graph in the figure above. The mean of the distribution, in our example the 80 kilos, is represented by the highest point right in the middle of the bell shaped curve. Notice the line that connects that highest point to the horizontal line, where it is marked 0. To the right of the zero, you will see +1σ, +2σ, +3σ and +4σ. To the left of the zero you will see the symmetrical values of -1σ, -2σ, -3σ and -4σ. What these notations show is the distance to the mean in terms of the standard deviation, which is 5 kilos in our example. Now notice the percentages that are shown inside the graph. For instance, in both the -1σ to 0 and the 0 to +1σ intervals, you will see written 34,13%. This is the normal distribution telling us that roughly 68% of all the people in the population weighs between 75 and 85 kilos. That's the mean of 80 kilos plus or minus one standard deviation of 5 kilos. Look at the scale at the very bottom of the figure which shows cumulative percentages. It tells us that 50%

of the people in the village weigh 80 kilos or less and 84% of the people weigh 85 kilos or less. In other words, 50% of the people weigh the same or less than the mean, and 84% of the people weigh the same or less than the mean plus one standard deviation. Ok…, you say, and how does knowing this weight stuff help us trade binary options? Glad you've asked, that's exactly what comes next.

Touch contracts

Touch contracts can in reality be *Touch* or *No Touch* contracts. Let's start with the first possibility. A touch contract is one that you win if the market touches the barrier that you have chosen at any time during the contract period. Emphasis on *at any time* during the contract period. You select a barrier and if the price of the asset touches that barrier *at any tim*e before the end date of the contract you will win the payout. With the *No Touch* variety you win only if the price *never* touches the barrier *at any time* during the contract period. It is at this point that what we know about the normal distribution comes handy. Here is how it works: we select as barrier the open of the first day of the contract plus one standard deviation above the mean variation to the highest value. Wow, that's a mouthful isn't it? Let's take one step back and go slowly.

We start as always by looking at what happened in the past. We measure the difference from the open price on the first day of the contract to the highest point it reaches during the contract period. We then calculate that difference as a percentage of the open price. We repeat this process for all the years for which we have data. As an example, suppose that in the first year for which you have data the open price is 80. The price rises to a maximum of 88 during the contract period. So in that year the distance from the opening to the highest point was 8 points. Expressed as a percentage of the open price that is 10%. You repeat these calculations for all the other years for which you have data. You will get something like 3%, 5%, 2%, -1%, -2%, 12%, etc. Next you calculate the mean and the standard deviation of those variations. Better yet, you let Excel or some other spreadsheet do it, they are really good at it. Recall that the normal distribution tells us that in 84% of the cases the variation from the beginning of the day of the contract to its higher point will be equal to or less than the mean variation plus one standard deviation. Suppose that the mean variation is 5% and that the standard deviation is 3%. If you set the barrier at 8%, you expect to win a No Touch contract 84% of the times, losing 26% percent of the times. Conversely you expect to win a Touch contract 26% of the times and post a loss 84% of the times.

Let's see an example of this for the month of May Calends strategy, using the S&P 500 index.

For the No Touch contract research shows that the magic number is 5%. By magic number what is meant is the average variation for the period plus one standard deviation, as we have seen. This is the percentage that you add to the open price to calculate your barrier. If the open price in May was 1000, you would add to it 5% which is 50, and set your barrier at 1050. Doing so in the past has resulted in a win 77% of the times. That's different from the theoretical 84% because you have but a few years of data and theoretical values always assume very large samples. So you build on the theory but then filter by the reality of your samples. The past shows a 77% win rate and that is what you take as the expected winning probability for a No Touch bet in the S&P500 with the barrier set as the opening price plus 5%. Now the question becomes "what is the minimum return you should accept for entering this trade"? Naturally, that has to be the return that will result in a positive expectancy for the trade. So you pull out the expectancy formula which is

Expectancy = reward to risk X win ratio – loss ratio

and you solve for the value that equals expectancy to zero. Your equation in this example would be the following:

0 = reward to risk X 77% – 23%

As with binary options you are always risking 100% of your stake the *reward to risk* here will be equal to the required return. Solving the equation you arrive at 0,2987 or roughly 30%. That is the return that makes the expectancy for this trade to be zero. Of course you do not want to trade it at that level but anything above it goes: 32%, 40%, 50%, etc. Once you know the exact return offered you calculate how much to stake using your money management system rules.

For this same example the Touch contract has the same magic number of 5% and of course is has the complementary probability of 23%. The minimum return is thus calculated using:

0 = reward to risk X 23% – 77%

That results in 3,3478 or roughly 335%. You will only enter this trade if they offer you a return above that.

Lane contracts

The lane contracts are those that have not one but two barriers. I refer to them as Lane contracts but actually a more common name is In/Out contracts at least that's the name Binary.com calls them.

In / Out – Ends Between/Outside

The In/Out contract come in two forms, the one that we'll look at first is the Ends Between / Ends Outside variation. With Ends Between contracts you win if the *exit spot price* is lower than the high barrier and higher than the low barrier. With the Ends Outside variation, you win if the exit spot is either higher than the high Barrier or lower than the low barrier. Again, it's only the *exit spot*, also referred to as the exit price or the price at the close of the last day of the contract period that matters.

Using a procedure similar to the one before, this time we make two calculations. We first compute the mean variation and the standard variation for those times when the exit spot is below the entry spot, that is to say the negative variations. We set the low barrier as the open price of the first day of the contract minus one standard deviation of those negative mean variations. We then compute the mean variation and the standard variation for those times when the exit spot is above the entry spot, that is to say the positive variations.

Let's see an example of this for the month of December Calends strategy, using the S&P 500 index. Research shows that you should set the low barrier subtracting 1.6% from the opening price and set the high barrier by adding 4.9% to it. If the open price in December was

1000 the low barrier would therefore be 984 and the high barrier would be 1049. Ends Between contracts thus set won 74% of the times in the past. Naturally that winning percentage drops to 26% with the Ends Outside variation. The minimum return acceptable for each one of these bet has to be above, respectively of 35% and 285%.

I want to draw your attention to one important psychological factor. Although the above Ends Between and Ends Outside bets are equivalent in terms of the expected result, in reality very few people will be able to play the Ends Outside game. That is because it entails losing three times out of four on average. Not many people can stomach that. Folks get nervous when they lose a couple of trades and it takes a special type of person to play to lose most of the time. The vast majority of traders will opt to go with the trades that have a higher winning percentage and will stay away from the ones that have a lower winning percentage.

In / Out – Stays Between / Goes Outside

With the Stays Between variation of the In/Out contract you will win if the price of the asset does not touch either the high or the low barrier *at any time* during the contract period. If you select the Goes Outside variation you win if it touches or goes outside the high or low barrier *at any time* during the contract period. The operative expression here is *any time* and this is what marks the difference to the Ends Between / Ends Outside type of contract where only what happens at the very end matters.

To know where to set the barriers we again split our calculations into two, one dealing with the negative variations and the other taking care of the positive variations. The difference is that in this case we compute the variations to the lowest and highest spots, not to the exit spots.

Looking at the S&P 500 Index for December research tells us to set the low barrier as the open minus 3.8% and the high barrier as the open plus 5.7%. We expect to win 71% of the times if we pick the Stays Between variation, with our minimum acceptable return being 40%. With the Goes Outside bet we only expect to win about 29% of the time so our minimum return is a much higher 250%.

The next section contains the data and research used in the examples presented in this book. Please be aware that the information is displayed after rounding and that may cause you to arrive at different results when trying to replicate some of the calculations.

To claim you reader bonus go to morbat.com/fivf.

S&P500 research

Time-based strategies

CALENDS				
Month	**Direction**	**Win %**	**Expectancy**	**Kelly**
January	Higher	62.9%	0.07	10%
February	Higher	60.0%	0.02	3%
March	Higher	68.6%	0.17	24%
April	Higher	68.6%	0.17	24%
May	Higher	62.9%	0.07	10%
June	Lower	51.4%	-0.13	0%
July	Lower	54.3%	-0.08	0%
August	Higher	60.0%	0.02	3%
September	Lower	51.4%	-0.13	0%
October	Higher	68.6%	0.17	24%
November	Higher	65.7%	0.12	17%
December	Higher	71.4%	0.21	31%

FOUR SEASONS				
Quarter	**Direction**	**Win %**	**Expectancy**	**Kelly**
January to March	Higher	65.7%	0.12	17%
April to June	Higher	65.7%	0.12	17%
July to September	Higher	60.0%	0.02	3%
October to December	Higher	80.0%	0.36	51%

TRIPLE WITCHING WEEKS				
Period	**Direction**	**Win %**	**Expectancy**	**Kelly**
Monday to 3rd Friday of March	Higher	51.2%	-0.13	0%
Monday to 3rd Friday of June	Lower	53.7%	-0.09	0%
Monday to 3rd Friday of September	Lower	52.5%	-0.11	0%
Monday to3rd Friday of December	Higher	56.1%	-0.05	0%

THANKSGIVING				
Period	**Direction**	**Win %**	**Expectancy**	**Kelly**
Monday to Friday after 4th Thursday of November	Higher	67.4%	0.15	21%

SELL IN MAY AND GO AWAY				
Period	**Direction**	**Win %**	**Expectancy**	**Kelly**
November to April	Higher	74.4%	0.26	38%

JANUARY BAROMETER				
Period	**Direction**	**Win %**	**Expectancy**	**Kelly**
February to December	Lower	33.3%	-0.43	0%
February to December	Higher	78.1%	0.33	47%

Touch / No Touch contracts

^GSPC: USA: S&P 500					
	Month's open +	No Touch		Touch	
Month	High	Win%	Min. Return	Win%	Min. Return
January	6.2%	89%	13%	11%	775%
February	4.6%	80%	25%	20%	400%
March	7.0%	91%	9%	9%	1067%
April	5.5%	89%	13%	11%	775%
May	5.0%	77%	30%	23%	338%
June	4.4%	80%	25%	20%	400%
July	5.1%	83%	21%	17%	483%
August	5.5%	86%	17%	14%	600%
September	5.0%	74%	35%	26%	289%
October	7.6%	91%	9%	9%	1067%
November	5.7%	83%	21%	17%	483%
December	5.7%	89%	13%	11%	775%

In / Out – Ends Between/Outside contracts

^GSPC: USA: S&P 500						
	Month's open +/-		ENDS BETWEEN		ENDS OUTSIDE	
Month	Low	High	Win%	Min. Return	Win%	Min. Return
January	-3.7%	5.7%	69%	46%	31%	218%
February	-3.9%	4.1%	74%	35%	26%	289%
March	-3.1%	5.2%	77%	30%	23%	338%
April	-1.9%	4.7%	69%	46%	31%	218%
May	-3.3%	4.7%	66%	52%	34%	192%
June	-3.1%	3.2%	71%	40%	29%	250%
July	-3.6%	4.2%	63%	59%	37%	169%
August	-4.9%	5.0%	69%	46%	31%	218%
September	-5.2%	3.7%	66%	52%	34%	192%
October	-5.5%	7.3%	86%	17%	14%	600%
November	-2.9%	5.2%	77%	30%	23%	338%
December	-1.6%	4.9%	74%	35%	26%	289%

In / Out – Stays Between / Goes Outside

^GSPC: USA: S&P 500						
Month	Month's open +/-		STAYS BETWEEN		GOES OUTSIDE	
Month	Low	High	Win%	Min. Return	Win%	Min. Return
January	-6.2%	6.2%	74%	35%	26%	289%
February	-5.1%	4.6%	66%	52%	34%	192%
March	-5.4%	7.0%	80%	25%	20%	400%
April	-4.3%	5.5%	80%	25%	20%	400%
May	-5.1%	5.0%	63%	59%	37%	169%
June	-4.4%	4.4%	66%	52%	34%	192%
July	-6.1%	5.1%	74%	35%	26%	289%
August	-7.4%	5.5%	77%	30%	23%	338%
September	-7.2%	5.0%	60%	67%	40%	150%
October	-10.7%	7.6%	86%	17%	14%	600%
November	-7.0%	5.7%	74%	35%	26%	289%
December	-3.8%	5.7%	71%	40%	29%	250%

About the author

José Manuel Moreira Batista is a private trader and investor and manages private concerns. After graduating in Business Administration in 1982 he did a stint in the Air Force and then went on to hold executive positions in several multinational corporations until 1999.

That year he left the corporate world and started the management consulting and training company that he still owns today. He also taught university courses in Corporate Finance, Financial Accounting, Cost Accounting and Real Estate.

As an early display of his uncanny market timing he started trading the stock market in 1987. In case you are wondering, he did not lose money in the crash having been ~~lucky~~ savvy enough to exit all his positions a few days before Monday, October 19. He kept actively trading, studying and researching throughout the years.

His results-oriented books and courses blend experience with a sound theoretical foundation to deliver practical, easy-to-follow knowledge that brings immediate benefits to readers and students.

Disclaimer

The author and the publisher make no representations as to the accuracy, completeness, suitability or validity of any information in this book and will not be liable for any errors or omissions in this information or any damages arising from its display or use. The author and the publisher are neither providing investment advisory services nor acting as registered investment advisors or broker-dealers; they also do not purport to tell or suggest which securities or currencies anyone should buy or sell for themselves. The author and the publisher may hold positions in the stocks, currencies or industries discussed here. You understand and acknowledge that there is a very high degree of risk involved in trading and that the author and the publisher assume no responsibility or liability for your trading and investment results.

It should not be assumed that the methods, techniques, or indicators presented will be profitable or that they will not result in losses. Past results of any individual trader or trading system are not indicative of future returns by that trader or system, and are not indicative of future returns which may be realized by you. In addition, the indicators, strategies, writings, workbooks, spreadsheets, check lists; blueprints etc. are provided for informational and educational purposes only and should not be construed as investment or trading advice. You should not rely solely on the information provided in making any investment. Rather, you should use it only as a starting point for your own independent research in order to allow you to form your own opinion regarding trading and investments. In addition, you should always check with your licensed financial advisor and tax advisor to determine the suitability of any trading or investment.

HYPOTHETICAL OR SIMULATED PERFORMANCE RESULTS HAVE CERTAIN INHERENT LIMITATIONS. UNLIKE AN ACTUAL PERFORMANCE RECORD, SIMULATED RESULTS DO NOT REPRESENT ACTUAL TRADING AND MAY NOT BE IMPACTED BY BROKERAGE AND OTHER SLIPPAGE FEES. ALSO, SINCE THE TRADES HAVE NOT ACTUALLY BEEN EXECUTED, THE RESULTS MAY HAVE UNDER- OR OVER-COMPENSATED FOR THE IMPACT, IF ANY, OF CERTAIN MARKET FACTORS, SUCH AS LACK OF LIQUIDITY. SIMULATED TRADING PROGRAMS IN GENERAL ARE ALSO SUBJECT TO THE FACT THAT THEY ARE DESIGNED WITH THE BENEFIT OF HINDSIGHT. NO REPRESENTATION IS BEING MADE THAT ANY ACCOUNT WILL OR IS LIKELY TO ACHIEVE PROFITS OR LOSSES SIMILAR TO THOSE SHOWN.

The author or the publisher may have an affiliate relationship with all or some of the companies whose products or services are mentioned. This means that, at no additional cost to you, the author or the publisher may earn a commission or credit if you decide to buy any of their products or services.